Makeovers for Your Outdoor Spaces

COUNTRY LIVING
EASY TRANSFORMATIONS

Makeovers for Your Outdoor Spaces

Backyards, Decks, Patios, Porches & Terraces

Elizabeth S. Hamilton

HEARST BOOKS
A Division of Sterling Publishing Co., Inc.
New York

A Primrose Productions Book
Designed by Stephanie Stislow

Library of Congress Cataloging-in-Publication Data

Hamilton, Elizabeth S.
    Country living easy transformations : makeovers for your outdoor spaces / Elizabeth S. Hamilton.
        p. cm.
    Includes index.
    ISBN-13: 978-1-58816-501-5
    ISBN-10: 1-58816-501-9
    1. Outdoor living spaces—Decoration.   I. Country living (New York, N.Y.) II. Title. III. Title: Easy transformations.
    NK2117.O87H36 2006
    747.7'9—dc22

                                                2006020843

10 9 8 7 6 5 4 3 2 1

Published by Hearst Books
A Division of Sterling Publishing Co., Inc.
387 Park Avenue South, New York, NY 10016

Country Living and Hearst Books are trademarks owned by Hearst Communications, Inc.

www.countryliving.com

For information about custom editions, special sales, premium and corporate purchases, please contact
Sterling Special Sales Department at 800-805-5489 or specialsales@sterlingpub.com.

Distributed in Canada by Sterling Publishing
c/o Canadian Manda Group, 165 Dufferin Street
Toronto, Ontario, Canada M6K 3H6

Distributed in Australia by Capricorn Link (Australia) Pty. Ltd.
P.O. Box 704, Windsor, NSW 2756 Australia

Manufactured in China

Sterling   ISBN 13: 978-1-58816-501-5
              ISBN 10: 1-58816-501-9

Contents

Foreword

For many of us, the garden is an escape from the fast pace of our daily lives—a special place we can go to relax, renew, and reconnect with nature. Far more than merely an attractive frame for our homes, the garden has become an extension of the house itself. In these outdoor "rooms" we can enjoy a cup of coffee and the morning paper, pursue a pastime, be alone with our thoughts, or entertain family and friends.

Decorating a garden is a lot like designing an interior. In both cases, making the most of the space you have, meeting your family's needs, and creating a look that captures your personal style are the goals. Where to begin is often the biggest challenge. In *Country Living Easy Transformations: Makeovers for Your Outdoor Spaces*, we've gathered dozens of idea-filled gardens to inspire you. There are welcoming porches, well-appointed patios, meandering paths, and secluded spots perfect for afternoon idylls. Whether you have a small courtyard or acres of land, this book will help you transform your garden into a retreat all your own.

NANCY MERNIT SORIANO
Editor-in-Chief
Country Living

LEFT: A lovingly tended, lush garden surrounds this cottage. Note the vintage garden tools that are used as finials atop the fenceposts.

Introduction

Today's outdoor spaces are designed for living—put simply, they extend the living areas of our homes out-of-doors. Once, we separated our homes into house and garden, each unto itself, with certain functions designated for indoors and others for outdoors. Nowadays, those boundaries have blurred and we seek to create spaces that flow gracefully into each other. We aim to live in a way that both connects us to our natural surroundings and allows us to enjoy all our available living space. The rewarding result of all this melding is the increasingly popular outdoor room, an easy-living space that is at once part of nature and of the home.

The outdoor room serves multiple purposes. It connects a home to its environment; creates a private space for residents and guests to enjoy the natural world; and encourages us to fully inhabit the space outside the house, whether we are strolling along a path, relaxing on a porch, or simply sitting on a bench contemplating patterns of sunlight and shadow.

The definition of an outdoor room is flexible, but, in essence, what makes an outdoor room recognizable as such is some way of defining the space that differentiates it from the rest of the outdoors—while still maintaining its harmony with the whole, of course. This may be done with walls, floors, roofs, plantings, containers, furnishings, and accessories, alone or in creative combinations.

Every sector of your outdoor space is eligible, regardless of its size and shape. Front yards, from the sidewalk to the front door, are a great place to start; aim for a welcoming approach to the house and a pleasing entryway. Side and backyard spaces, such as porches, patios, and decks, make appealing transitions from indoors to out. Outdoor rooms can also emerge as you move farther away from the house, using paths and walkways that are essentially outdoor corridors, to partially or fully enclosed spaces framed by fences and walls. Freestanding structures, such as pergolas and arbors, give definition to expansive areas. Even something as simple and transient as a picnic blanket can create a fresh-air room for a moment in time.

The outdoor rooms in this book interpret the concept in all sorts of wonderful ways. Let them inspire you to transform your outdoor space into an integral, irresistible, and essential part of your home.

LEFT: A pair of chairs transforms a corner into a destination.

Welcoming Impressions

An appealing, functional front yard is an integral component of any home—think of it as the out-of-doors portion of your vestibule or foyer. Since it provides everyone who comes to your door with a first impression of your home, it has an important public role to play; but do not design the front of your home just to impress visitors—it should welcome *you* home, too, smoothing your transition from public space to private space.

A welcoming front yard design draws visitors toward the home, enlivening the path to the door. It should reflect the style and scale of your home, emphasizing the design elements that define your home's personality, and it should be functional as an entryway, that is, a place where people pause on their way indoors.

Many front yards were originally designed simply to offer a largely unobstructed view of the home's architecture, with easy access to the front door and perhaps some plantings to obscure the meeting point of façade and foundation. Today's homeowners prefer to consider their front yard an essential part of the home's living area. The front yards in this chapter offer clever solutions and creative ideas that reveal how, with a little imagination, it is simple to transform a plain front yard into one that projects warmth and personality and invites family, friends, and visitors to linger at the threshold and enjoy the welcome.

LEFT: This green-and-periwinkle cottage features a front porch leading to an outdoor room that has been designed to flatter the home. Here, the classic combination of picket fence and arched gateway has a curvy line that softens the straight lines of the home's frame. A pale green paint links the façade and fence, creating a unified feeling for the whole space.

LEFT: A harmonious palette draws together all the elements of this appealing bungalow's front area. The warm terra-cotta tiles of the walkway and patio were selected to reflect the home's primary color, while the contrasting trim colors are repeated in random spots from the chair outside the front door to the trellis to the flower beds. This outdoor vestibule is friendly, cheerful, and casual, a combination continued inside the home.

A WEATHERED WORKTABLE AND A SET OF PEGS BY THE DOOR GIVE THIS OUTDOOR SPACE UNIQUE CHARACTER, WHILE AT THE SAME TIME MAKING IT VERY FUNCTIONAL.

ABOVE : Foundation plantings and curvaceous beds delineate the outdoor area in front of this neat and trim historic saltbox house. Rows of carefully trimmed, rounded shrubs emphasize the home's balanced proportions, while a less formal bed curves around the expansive lawn, creating a defined area that's perfect for a leisurely stroll amid the plantings.

ABOVE: A pebbled walkway invites visitors to wander and enjoy the embellishments that grace the front yard of this home. By placing urns and statuary at strategic points among the flowers and trees, the home's owners have created several spots where one can linger before reaching the front door. A veranda overlooking the garden provides another outdoor space from which to enjoy views of the greenery.

LEFT: The teal-and-red color scheme of this Greek Revival home works with the lush, colorful plantings lining the path to create a peaceful, soothing outdoor space. Visitors are encouraged by a simple, yet prominently displayed bench to sit and appreciate their surroundings while relaxing in the shade of the tree.

ABOVE: A modern dooryard garden recalls Colonial outdoor rooms where the lady of the house traditionally spent hours in her vegetable and cutting gardens. Here a whitewashed fence encloses the front yard—an effective way to delineate an outdoor room—and pebbled pathways lead the way through the garden. A gate differentiates the front porch from the garden room.

ABOVE: This country cottage announces its intention to please both eye and spirit by transforming its driveway into an *allée* of sorts that offers several equally appealing destinations. Following the path all the way leads to a whitewashed arch that frames the yard and studio (formerly a garage) beyond. Midway down the path, a pair of white urns announces a detour to a table and chairs set under the trees. A wooden stair opposite, almost camouflaged by abundant greenery, leads to the front entrance. Though the effect is of three distinct rooms, the use of white paint, furnishings, and flowers unifies the whole yard.

PLACING AN ARCH AT THE END, RATHER THAN THE BEGINNING, OF A PATHWAY LENGTHENS THE VISUAL SPACE AND MAKES AN OUTDOOR ROOM SEEM LONGER.

ABOVE: This historic townhouse, despite a tiny front yard, enjoys an outdoor vestibule created by claiming and framing the space that exists. A picket fence encloses the area, while a rose-draped arch frames the doorway and adds a sense of height. A pair of potted shrubs extends the walkway onto the sidewalk, effectively lengthening the path to the door.

RIGHT: A sheltered front patio protects this outdoor space from the elements, providing an appealing alcove to one side of the front door. The curved beds planted around a winding path offer contrast to the geometric lines of the house and lead to a bench that invites visitors to stop and sit a while.

LEFT: This small stoop projects enormous charm. The doorway architecture is distinguished by its symmetry, which is echoed in the pair of chairs that sits on each side of the door, a duo of vintage urns set on raised concrete pedestals, and two abundant floral beds lining either side of the central path. Each successive pairing gently draws the visitor toward the door.

Outdoor Lighting 101

Outdoor rooms, like their indoor counterparts, need several kinds of illumination.

Ambient Lighting: This is the overall glow that illuminates the space in general. Some examples include an overhead, ceiling-mounted fixture on a porch; a pair of sconces situated to either side of a doorway; or a string of fairy lights laced through an arbor or hanging above a patio.

Walkway Lighting: Usually low-slung, these are the essential lights that provide visibility for walking areas, especially along paths and stairways. They come in many styles, from in-stair spots to solar lamps that can be staked right into the ground.

Focal-point Lighting: Focused and task-oriented, this kind of lighting is used to illuminate cooking and dining areas or to highlight decorative features such as fountains or statuary. Permanent lighting can come in the form of up- or down-spots; temporary choices include torches, hurricane lamps, and candles.

LEFT: With plenty of yard area around this charming Cape Cod–style cottage, there is room for both a semiprivate outdoor room in the front of the home and a more enclosed backyard. The two are linked by identical arched gateways at both ends of a brick path. A profusion of plantings on either side of the white fence obscures the view into the front yard while giving it a welcoming, country feeling.

DECORATIVE DETAILS MAKE A SIMPLE FRONT GATE SPECIAL. A DOUBLE ARCH GIVES THE STRUCTURE SUBSTANCE, AND THE CIRCLE FORMED BY THE CLOSED GATE CREATES AN ENCHANTING FRAME FOR THE VIEW. A PAIR OF FINIALS ATOP THE ARCH DRAWS THE EYE UPWARD TO THE CHARMING GABLED ROOF.

LEFT: Nature provided the approach to this barn-turned-home with a dramatic focal point—a massive old tree that dominates the space. In choosing to build a bench to surround the tree trunk, the homeowners have found a way to link this natural wonder with the home. The simple, white metal bench gently encloses the tree, and invites visitors to enjoy its natural beauty as they sit for a while under its shady canopy.

ABOVE: An entrance can achieve great style with a few special touches that elongate the approach to the home and frame the doorway. Here, a stone archway set with a wooden door adds drama and a sense of anticipation. Symmetrical plantings of varying heights, including two potted ficus trees placed midway along the walk and two more potted plants at the door, frame the entry and soften the transition from public to private space.

Porches

Practically a synonym for "relaxation," the porch is the easiest outdoor room to create. A natural extension of the home, easily accessed and sheltered from the elements, the porch offers outdoor living at its most effortless.

So what are the design challenges of this outdoor room? With a roof, railings, and columns, the space is already defined. The trick lies in making the porch both stylish and functional. A great porch does two things well—it reflects both the style of the home and the lifestyle of the people who live there.

A porch, whether front, side, or back, connects home and yard both visually and physically. The style of the porch and its décor should suit the look and scale of the house and the surrounding environment, so that the transition from indoors to outdoors is seamless and natural.

Equally important, as an open-air living area, the porch must incorporate the interests and activities of the home's dwellers, so it becomes a place to which everyone naturally gravitates and where they feel comfortable spending time.

The porches in this chapter accomplish these things via a variety of creative approaches. They reveal the different ways people enjoy outdoor living, from those who like to dine and entertain alfresco to those for whom the porch is a place to find tranquility and repose.

SCREENING IN A PORCH CAN DRAMATICALLY INCREASE THE OPPORTUNITY TO ENJOY IT, ADDING AN EXTRA MEASURE OF PROTECTION FROM THE WEATHER AND ANY LOCAL WILDLIFE.

LEFT: A rustic cottage boasts a cozy porch that beckons with a mix of vintage furnishings and comfy seating that perfectly reflects the old-fashioned feel of the building itself.

Try This Idea

A painted floor adds instant style to a porch. Several paint manufacturers make special paints intended for high-traffic outdoor areas—porch paints—two coats of which will make a durable surface. Some ideas to try:

• Stripes are a summery staple because they create a fresh, lively look. Opt for white with blue or green for a cool feeling; choose neutrals for a tranquil ambience.

• A checkerboard pattern is an old favorite for a painted floor. Try black and white for old-fashioned farmhouse charm or use dark and light shades of wood stain to let the beauty of a wooden floor show through.

• Gingham, though a country classic, makes for an unusual floor treatment. Its geometric pattern is perfect for a floor.

• Stencils make it easy to paint a floor with a variety of motifs. Some popular choices include florals, farm animals, and aphorisms.

RIGHT: A small porch has big personality when dressed up for the season with leaves and gourds from the yard. Simply furnished with a rustic table and an eclectic mix of chairs, this porch can be easily embellished for any occasion, in this case, an autumn feast. Its spare yet thoughtful design works without added decoration, too.

THE TREE-BRANCH RAILINGS FIND A NATURAL MATCH IN THE TABLE LEGS—A SUBTLE BUT DISTINCTIVE DECORATIVE TOUCH.

LEFT: A relaxing paradise of wicker and greenery, this back porch blurs the border between house and garden. A checkerboard wooden floor, painted to resemble green slate, picks up the leafy atmosphere and the floral pattern on the vintage-style seating. Conveniences such as a magazine holder, standing lamp, and a small table for refreshments are quiet and unobtrusive, contributing to the overall effect of a green and tranquil garden room.

AN UNFINISHED FLOOR LENDS
A RUSTIC, CASUAL TOUCH.

LEFT: This charming front porch puts forward a
welcoming air. Sidewalk planters and stairside beds draw
visitors toward the door; their symmetry mimicks that
of the home's architectural style. Narrow but spanning the
length of the house, the porch offers much in the way of
comfort, including a swing with plenty of cushions and
occasional tables to hold beverages and treats.

ABOVE: A wide back porch gently gives way to a
meadowlike yard by keeping its furnishings simple and
its views unobstructed. Made for relaxing, this porch is
furnished with mismatched wicker and a small table.
The striped and flowered cushions provide comfort; the
pastoral scenery does the rest.

LEFT: A red-and-white color scheme gives this porch its polish. At once whimsical and sophisticated, this look works because it is kept simple. The deep red of the house is repeated in the benches with bright white as an accent. The quilts make charming table covers that bring unity to the design.

ONE APPLE CANDLE IS A CUTE NOVELTY; A ROW OF THEM IS A DECORATIVE CELEBRATION OF THE SEASON.

RIGHT: A graceful wraparound porch evokes the pleasures of an era past. Lacy Victorian gingerbread sets the tone for this grand, old-fashioned porch, and its furnishings follow suit. In a mix much beloved by the Victorians, a combination of floral, patterned, and solid fabrics cover the cushions on the wicker furniture; a green-and-white palette brings it all together.

PLACE SEATING TO ENCOURAGE CONVERSATION BY GROUPING CHAIRS AND SOFA AROUND A CENTRAL, LOW TABLE.

Wicker Wisdom

Wicker is not a material itself; the word actually refers to furniture that is woven. A variety of materials may be woven into wicker, including:

Rattan: A climbing, solid-core vine found in Southeast Asia with a stem that is ⅛ to 2 inches (0.3 to 5 cm) wide; it grows to approximately 600 feet (183 m) long.

Cane: The stem of a large rattan plant.

Bamboo: A hollow-core grass of which there are more than 500 varieties.

Reed: Any swamp grass or rush that can be woven into furniture; this is the material most often used in vintage American wicker.

Willow: Tree branches, commonly used in European wicker.

Fiberglass resin: Frequently used today for its weather-resistant properties.

The earliest wicker dates to ancient times; both the Egyptians and Romans wove baskets and furnishings. Wicker achieved its peak popularity, however, during the Victorian period, in both Europe and the New World. Strong and versatile, it was used for all kinds of furniture, both indoor and outdoor, from cribs to armchairs.

To keep wicker clean, dust regularly with a soft cloth or brush; you may also vacuum it using the brush attachment. If it gets quite dirty, use a damp cloth to wipe it down.

If considering vintage wicker, be sure that the frame is in good condition, as this is the most difficult part to repair.

A MINIMOTIF OF STRIPES IS REPEATED
ON THE CUSHIONS AND THE LAMPSHADE.

LEFT: Nestled at one end of a back porch is a cozy dining spot. Tucking the table and chairs into the corner of the porch creates an area separate from the rest of the space, further removed by a curtain of morning glory vines and a screen of potted plants to create privacy. Hanging a vintage lantern above the table centers the room and provides a romantic ambience for evening (heightened by the silver candlesticks collected at each end). During the day, the table and chairs offer a pleasant spot for morning coffee or an outdoor lunch.

ABOVE: A front porch announces its flea-market ambience with a mix of wrought iron, wood, and wicker finds. The white background provides a simple backdrop for the varied pieces.

ABOVE: Roses cascade from a pergola-style roof to shield this porch from outside eyes. Exuberant plantings all around the porch create a natural, pleasing sense of enclosure, while still allowing light and breezes to come through.

LEFT: A pergola rather than a roof overhead contributes to the open, airy feeling of this expansive back porch. Neutral and natural in its use of color and uncluttered with extraneous furnishings and accessories, this porch features a long farmhouse table surrounded by comfortable wicker armchairs—the goal is to dine amid the natural beauty without distraction. A plain wooden fan overhead generates a little extra breeze on hot days.

DON'T FORGET THE DETAILS: A CEILING
FAN WILL KEEP THE BREEZES MOVING
ON EVEN THE HOTTEST DAYS, WHILE A
SPEAKER BRINGS MUSIC TO THE PORCH.

LEFT: Victorian details get an update on this lovely
screened-in porch. The chintz-covered cushions on wicker
chairs, a vintage settee upholstered in stripes, and an
ornate coffee table add up to a Victorian scene, but the
white paint and an absence of clutter bring the porch
into the modern era with a clean, crisp feeling.

ABOVE: This elegant open-air dining room shows
that outdoor décor can be every bit as sophisticated as
that found indoors—and it makes eating outside a daily
delight. A large, wooden dining table and comfortable
chairs ensure that guests are happy to sit through several
courses, while a side table makes service easy. A durable
bamboo area rug below the table grounds the dining area.
And a mirror placed on the house wall reflects the view
and the light, adding to the pleasure of this beautifully
executed outdoor room.

Patios and Decks

Patios and decks, among the most popular and versatile of outdoor spaces, are easy to create in almost any kind of yard. A patio or deck may be attached to the home or be entirely freestanding.

A deck is typically built out from the house, incorporating one of the outside walls in its structure. If the deck is raised above ground level, it is likely to have railings as well—these confining features help to give it definition. A patio is unconfined; it may blend seamlessly into the surrounding landscape or have borders of plantings or furnishings.

A key consideration for both patio and deck is flooring material, and there are styles and shapes galore to choose from. Wood, stone, concrete, and brick are all options, each giving a unique flavor to the space.

Seating is the next choice, and before proceeding with this aspect of your design, you should determine how you will use this outdoor space. Alfresco dining is one of the most delightful activities accommodated by a patio or deck; as the photographs in this chapter reveal, there are dozens of creative expressions of outdoor dining rooms. Or perhaps you long for a patio or deck on which to engage in less social pursuits—quiet contemplation, reading, gardening, or simply appreciating the view. Whatever your desire, you will need to select the lounges, chairs, tables, and accessories that fulfill your idea of easy outdoor living.

LEFT: An arched gate, painted a warm red, provides a dramatic entryway to this inviting outdoor dining room. Tucked against the house, this small patio room obtains an intimate feeling from the embrace of the walls created by the fence, the home itself, and the abundant greenery.

LEFT: The transition from home to garden is seamless at this serene cottage where a pebbled patio segues into a path through the flower beds. A trio of doors forms the back "wall" of this garden room, while the pebbled flooring defines the social spaces. Effortless and simple, this patio needs only a table and chairs to become an elegant outdoor dining room.

PEBBLES ARE AN EASY-CARE AND VERSATILE FLOORING MATERIAL, PERFECT FOR CREATING A CASUAL FEELING.

A POND WITH A MINIFOUNTAIN
BRINGS THE SOOTHING SOUND
OF WATER INTO THE ROOM.

LEFT: Bordered on one side by the house, this flagstone patio opens onto a grassy backyard. A trellised "doorway" has been placed to one side, providing another border as well as framing the view both into and beyond the dining area. The placement of the table gives the best view of the gently sloping yard, while making the most of the available patio space.

ABOVE: A backyard patio blends Mexican influences with flea-market eclecticism for a colorful and relaxing outdoor room. With walls on two sides and a floor of plain pavers, this large patio offers plenty of room for fun. A dining area features a wrought-iron table and chairs, painted white and adorned with fabric featuring a bovine motif. Benches and chairs in a variety of styles are scattered around the patio, draped with colorful Mexican blankets, inviting guests to relax. The effect is one of casual welcome, with lots of special comfortable touches.

A B O V E : Stone and tile come together for a durable and stylish
terrace that descends in several levels from the French doors of this
Arts-and-Crafts-influenced home. Keeping the look simple and natural,
a pair of iron urns sets off the doorway.

Try This Idea

Porch and patio doors are important elements of both the design and the décor. As visual transitions between indoor and outdoor rooms, they offer great opportunities for stylish touches. A few ideas to try:

• Old-fashioned screen doors with fretwork or gingerbread

• Unusual styles, such as Dutch doors (top and bottom open separately)

• Double-wide French doors

• Stained-glass windows in the door itself or in the transom or sidelights

• Vintage doors repainted or refinished

• Decorative treatments on the windowpanes, such as etching

• Vintage or old-fashioned door hardware

• Decorative light fixtures—a single fixture above or sconces placed on either side of the door

• Decorative painting on moldings and trim

ABOVE: A small side patio has been carved from the forest floor and "paved" with environmentally friendly nutshells. A folding table and chairs can be set up to take advantage of a sunny day or quickly put away if the weather turns unfriendly.

LEFT: Perched high on a forested slope, this cottage features a deck that is a true extension of the indoor living space. Large, wide-open doors make the wall of the cottage virtually disappear, and an over-hanging roof provides partial protection from the elements. The extended part of the deck boasts a pair of Adirondack chairs, placed for optimum enjoyment of the view.

BRICK PAVERS ENGRAVED WITH
DESIGNS MAKE AN OUT-OF-
THE-ORDINARY PATIO BASE.

ABOVE: A low stone wall embraces a brick patio that is a wonderful destination reached by following the paths of this large, beautifully landscaped garden. Accessed by flagstone stairs and encircled by plantings that soften its edges, this patio is the focal point of the yard. Its only furnishings are an elaborate wrought-iron pedestal table and matching chairs, which form an elegant outdoor dining room.

MIX FLOORING MATERIALS FOR AN
ECLECTIC LOOK: BRICKWORK, GRAVEL,
AND WEATHERED WOOD ALL WORK
TOGETHER HERE IN A WAY THAT IS AT
ONCE RUSTIC YET SOPHISTICATED.

LEFT: A pleasing patio can be created from even a little bit of space. Here, just inside the gate and to one side of the front entrance, lies a small gravel patio. With a pair of chairs and a folding table, it yields a pleasant spot to sit; it also offers a showcase area for flea-market garden treasures, such as the birdbath, bunny ornament, and weathered pot.

LEFT: An old potting shed provides the backdrop to this charming patio, inspired by the classic English garden, where a variety of vintage treasures finds an outdoor home. A brickwork floor with the shiny patina of age features an armchair and side table set beneath a vine-wrapped pergola. Salvaged blue shutters and an oil painting of roses add a whimsical touch.

POTTED PLANTS ARE GREAT OUTDOOR DECORATING ELEMENTS—EASY TO CARE FOR, CHANGE, AND ARRANGE. USE THEM TO CREATE ACCENTS, FORM SCREENS, OR CHANGE THE MOOD.

LEFT: With plenty of retro-style metal lawn chairs determining the look, and a vintage toy tractor adding a touch of charm, this deck is both stylish and functional. Metal buckets hold drinks, one large table carries snacks, and occasional tables can be moved as needed. A big basket holds anything that is best kept out of the way.

Deck Materials

Decks are traditionally constructed of wood, but in today's technologically advanced world, there are also synthetic materials and blends to choose from.

Wood: Hardwoods are naturally durable and rot-resistant, which means they may be stained or left natural. Good hardwood deck choices include cedar, cypress, ironwood (also called ipe), and teak. Look for hardwood that has been logged from sustainable forests; avoid endangered forest species such as redwood. **Softwoods** are less expensive but must be treated for weather-resistance. Most pressure-treated lumber is pine or fir; ask for pressure-treated lumber that is certified free of toxic chemicals. Softwood decks will need to stained, and then regularly restained, in order to maintain durability—remember to choose an environmentally friendly stain.

Synthetics: Composites are blends of wood fibers (from waste wood) and plastics. They are very long-lasting and durable. **Vinyl lumber** is completely synthetic and extremely durable. None of the synthetic decking materials truly resemble wood, though they do come in wood tones and styles.

Patio Materials

When choosing your patio materials, there are two main criteria to keep in mind: appearance and stability. The patio should complement the house and landscape, fitting in attractively with its surroundings. The patio surface should be stable and reasonably flat—sufficiently so that a table and chairs can rest without wobbling. Numerous materials fit the bill:

Stone: Natural and strong, with variations in the surface. Good patio stone includes fieldstone, slate, limestone, flagstone, sandstone, and many others. The style can range from rustic to formal.

Gravel or pebbles: Slightly less stable but with good drainage; excellent for lining walkways.

Brick: Clay bricks are hard, flat, and durable and come in different grades based on climate. They can be laid in a variety of interesting patterns.

Concrete pavers: Hard, flat, and very long-lasting, concrete pavers come in different shapes that can be laid in interlocking patterns.

Tile: Comes in a wide range of shapes and colors; be sure to choose a tile that won't be slippery when wet.

Poured concrete: Today, poured concrete can be found in numerous textures, colors, and shapes, making it a very versatile and practical patio surface.

OUTDOOR STYLE IS NOT RULE-BOUND; A GARGOYLE MAY FIND A HAPPY HOME ON A MODERN DECK, PARTICULARLY IF ITS COLORING BLENDS WELL WITH THE SURROUNDINGS.

ABOVE: A small stone patio looks out on a panoramic view at this lakefront home. A low, wooden fence draws a clear distinction between yard and woods while abundant gardens provide a bit of added privacy.

LEFT: Spare and with clean lines, this deck has been designed to quietly blend with the magnificent green woodland beyond. With the custom-built benches and storage bins constructed from the same wood as the deck, all the planks have acquired the classic gray weathered color that does not detract from the view.

LEFT: This tranquil patio set under the trees features inset flower beds that break up the stone slabs, which have been allowed to settle just slightly askew. A single stone bench and a pedestal sundial with creepers growing around its base complete this outdoor room. The end result is a patio with the enchanted feeling of a secret garden growing a little bit wild.

ABOVE: An outdoor room emerges when a corner of this long lawn is sectioned off by placing concrete pavers in a checkerboard pattern in the grass. A vine-covered pergola defines the space above and around the patio, and together with a stone table and weathered chairs, gives an air of venerable age to this outdoor room.

RIGHT : Viewed from above, it is easy to see how this long backyard has been divided into three outdoor rooms, each merging into the next. Closest to the house, Saltillo-style tiles define a patio perfect for entertaining and dining. Beyond it, a two-level terrace with brick pavers in both herringbone and rectangular patterns is graced with four formal minigardens. The brick-paved stairs lead up to the top level, where an oval lawn ends in a potted garden.

ABOVE: White trelliswork encloses this back patio, creating an airy yet sheltered space. A mix of materials—iron, wood, and brick—is unified by a coat of whitewash, while a crystal chandelier dangles in front of a mirror, enhancing the play of light. The result is refined and sophisticated—with a touch of whimsy supplied by a bunny garden ornament and some topiary balls.

LEFT: With a pergola-style roof and walls on three sides, this alcove deck is already an outdoor room of sorts, but textiles transform it into a comfortable, colorful, fresh-air den. Rugs warm up the wooden floor, colorful pillows cushion the bench, and a crochet-hemmed cloth gives the folding table a stylish look. Drawing the blue-and-white draperies creates a fourth wall and turns this deck into an intimate outdoor hideaway.

JUST AS THEY DO INDOORS, COLLECTIONS PLACED OUTDOORS EXPRESS THE PASSIONS AND PERSONALITY OF THE HOMEOWNER. HERE, A COLLECTION OF OVERSIZED FINIALS ADDS A WHIMSICAL TOUCH.

ABOVE: Set slightly away from the house, this red brick patio has a relaxed and welcoming air. The edges are softened by an array of potted plants, which help merge the patio seamlessly into the greenery around it. Vintage seating, each piece unique, is placed facing inward to enhance conversation.

RIGHT: At the back of this home, a narrow wrap-around porch has been expanded to create a much larger, more useful outdoor space. A shaded dining area is set beneath the overhanging roof, while the deck extends outward past the original porch posts into a broad expanse with plenty of room for relaxing. The use of white as the main color, with just a few green accents, ensures that the deck integrates smoothly with the rest of the home's architecture.

RIGHT: Flea-market eclecticism makes for casual comfort on this welcoming deck. The slightly worn air shared by all the pieces makes the matching set of vintage garden bench and chair look right at home next to the fifties-era metal lawn chair. A Mexican blanket adds flashes of color.

ARCHITECTURAL ELEMENTS SALVAGED FROM OLD BUILDINGS MAKE UNIQUE PLANT STANDS AND/OR DECORATIVE ELEMENTS.

LEFT: A small, fenced-in patio becomes an elegant outdoor dining room when the space is filled with formal furniture that is both sophisticated and substantial. The whitewashed dining table holds the center, with a pair of refined upholstered chairs and a handsome bench providing seating on either side. The all-white palette continues with the addition of two planters; the basket of annuals offers a splash of pink for contrast.

Fences, Walls, and Gates

Walls and fences form the vertical architecture of outdoor rooms, giving shape to the space and creating privacy, often where none existed before. Their impact on the look of an outdoor space is hard to overstate; indeed, the materials and design of a fence or wall can set the style of the entire outdoor décor. Wooden styles vary widely within the ranges of solid to open and traditional to modern— there is plenty of room for interesting design here. Stone does lend a certain character to a wall, but even so, the design may be high, imposing, formal, low, friendly, or fanciful.

Walls and fences are also enormously versatile, and, when part of the design of an outdoor room, they can be used for practical purposes, such as to fix borders, block unwelcome sights and sounds, create privacy or intimacy, divide space, and form a transition from one area to another. They can also exist for purely decorative reasons, complementing the home's architecture, adding an accent, or drawing attention to an embellishment. The walls and fences in this chapter do all of these things in many creative ways.

Where there is a wall or fence, you will usually find a gate. Symbolic as well as functional, the gate is a uniquely significant architectural element, and it can be one of the most striking parts of any outdoor room.

LEFT: A long arbor forms a passageway from one area of the garden to the next. A gate set at the midpoint inspires the visitor to spend a moment under the canopy of roses, a brief stop in a tiny outdoor room created from wood, metal, and plant life.

ABOVE: An arched gateway topped with a rose-covered arbor frames an enchanting view at this lakefront hideaway. The small garden room gets its charm as much from the picture-perfect scenery as from the coziness created by the picket-fence enclosure.

RIGHT: White picket fencing encloses this front garden room that is distinguished by a tall birdhouse. The gateway, with its trellis-style walls and curved arbor, draws the visitor in and directs his or her gaze to the decorative roof and finial of the birdhouse.

ABOVE: A mix of styles comes together beautifully in this entrance to a roomy yard. A wooden fence is typically matched with a similarly rustic gate, but here, an imposing wrought-iron gate offers a startling and delightful contrast. Two small stone lions serve as modest guardians of this entryway to the area beyond.

LEAVING THE IRON GATES
SLIGHTLY AJAR CREATES
A MORE WELCOMING AIR.

ABOVE: An unusual gate is a destination in itself. Inspired by the twig furniture that graces the garden beyond it, this unique gate provides an intriguing entry point—and is a piece of artistry worth stopping to admire on the way in.

LEFT: A Victorian-style garden room benefits from a low stone wall that separates it from the waters of a pond while keeping the view in easy sight. Uneven and slightly weathered, the wall adds to the old-fashioned charm of the site.

WALLS CAN BE EMBELLISHED NOT ONLY WITH TRAILING PLANTS, SUCH AS THESE ROSES, BUT WITH OTHER ACCESSORIES, SUCH AS THE CHERUB ON A PEDESTAL TUCKED AGAINST THE STONE.

A RAISED FLOWER BED EASES
THE TRANSITION FROM THE
HIGH WALL INTO THE PEBBLED
PATIO AREA.

ABOVE: Two stone walls form a tiered border for this yard. The taller wall, formed from rounded stones in varying shades, is a solid, imposing backdrop that also delivers perfect privacy. Its grandiosity is tempered by the lower wall of flatter gray stones from which plants cascade, and on which the cat finds a pleasant perch.

LEFT: A rustic split-rail fence forms the border between a working garden and a relaxing backyard. Both functional and decorative, this type of fence clearly delineates the different areas while permitting plants to spill through and leaving the view wide open.

LEFT: A stone wall, even if it is newly built, can impart an air of venerable age because the material itself is ancient. To further the illusion, look for finishing touches that reflect times gone by, such as this medieval-looking door with its iron hinges.

LEFT: A low stone retaining wall contains the exuberant garden that fronts this small guest cottage. The seemingly casual placement of the stones reflects the informal style of the garden, with its mix of colorful flowers.

Wall Stones

Although there are hundreds of varieties of stone in as many hues, when building a wall, it is the shape of the stone that is most important.

If you are obtaining your stone from a stoneyard (rather than collecting it yourself from your environment), you'll find that there are three main shapes available for purchase:

Rounded: These stones, typically fieldstone, come in rounded or oval shapes. They are excellent for a rustic wall.

Stacked: These are mostly flat but may vary in shape, and work for a formal or casual look.

Dressed: These are flat and cut to be uniform in shape; they are ideal for a formal wall.

LEFT: Two kinds of fencing are at work in this formal garden room. A high, dense hedge forms a living fence that is both beautiful and effective as a privacy barrier and windscreen. At the same time, a low, decorative picket fence cordons off an inner area—and gets a touch of teal paint for added visual interest.

FOR YEAR-ROUND PRIVACY, CHOOSE AN EVERGREEN HEDGE (GOOD CHOICES INCLUDE YEW, BOXWOOD, HOLLY, JUNIPER, AND ARBORVITAE)— AND LEARN TO PRUNE PROPERLY TO MAINTAIN FULLNESS.

RIGHT: An old bell announces visitors to the abundant cottage garden that forms a welcoming outdoor room for this house in the country. A scalloped picket fence, once bright white, has been allowed to fade a bit, and its weathered charm sets a relaxed tone for the space. The low, windowpane-style gate is another informal touch.

Try This Idea

Distinguish your picket fence with one of these distinctive touches:

• Choose a scalloped or other curvaceous shape instead of a continuous row of same-height pickets.

• Add finials to the tops of the posts—spears, points, and balls are all possibilities—or use vintage finials.

• Paint it any color but white; or go multicolored with pickets in different but complementary hues.

Paths and Destinations

Much of the pleasure to be gained from an outdoor room is the enjoyment of getting there; that is why landscape designers frequently incorporate paths and walkways that lead to outdoor destinations. Any outdoor space can be transformed by the inclusion of a focal point (or more than one) and a path to reach it.

There truly is no limit to an outdoor room's focal point save your imagination; it might be as simple and passive as a pretty view or as complex and active as a boxwood labyrinth. It might be a Victorian gazing ball hidden among the flowers; a bench positioned under a vine-entwined arbor; an old, mossy birdbath found at a flea market; or a picnic table laden with freshly grilled treats. It is up to you to decide what works in your space and with your outdoor lifestyle.

Paths and walkways do have some rules. They must be accessible, visible, and stable to walk on. They do not need to follow the shortest route from one point to another, however, and the best paths are interesting to walk in themselves, stimulating all the senses, and making the destination a bonus. The outdoor rooms in this chapter embrace the concept of the journey and offer many splendid reasons for adding a walkway and destination to your outdoor space.

L E F T : Moss grows on this woodland walkway constructed from local stone set into the earth. A sort of outdoor hallway that winds through stands of birch, this curving path proves more interesting to the eye than a straight one.

A PATH CAN SIMPLY WIND TO AN END, AS THIS ONE DOES, WITHOUT LOOPING BACK TO A STARTING POINT.

A B O V E : A hand-laid stone path diverts tranquility seekers off the main lawn to a spot perfect for a moment of quiet contemplation. Bordered by tall shrubs and grasses, this little alcove welcomes visitors with a gently weathered chair and an air of peacefulness.

ABOVE: Focal points can be seasonal, as is this dramatic magnolia tree coming into bloom in the springtime garden. A grassy path loops around the magnificent tree, offering a 360-degree view. A simple stone bench gives visitors a place to sit and inhale the sweet scent.

LEFT: This spectacular backyard abounds with destinations along a wide path. A profusely flowering bed separates it into two distinct rooms that are connected by a brick pathway running below a grapevine-covered arbor. Rectangular red bricks (which mimic the shapes of the beds and the garden itself) form the wide walkway; along the path are numerous stopping points, each one featuring something special to observe—on the outer perimeter, birdbaths and houses; on the inside, a small pond forming the focal point of the lower half of the garden. Strategically placed benches offer resting spots for taking in the sights.

UNOBTRUSIVE LIGHTS STAKED INTO THE FLOWER BEDS OFFER ILLUMINATION FOR EVENING WALKS.

A B O V E : The destination in this refined outdoor room is the antique pedestal sundial. It anchors the space, which is carefully designed to draw the eye from every vantage point toward the center. Framed in the background by the carefully clipped hedge (which shelters a wooden bench), it is also framed in the foreground by a leafy arbor that marks the entrance to the space. A grass path, lined with silvery sage, leads to the sundial, which presides over a circular bed.

R I G H T : The detailed metalwork of a vintage urn resting on a pedestal is on view in this quiet garden room. A brick path is patterned at right angles and in circles to lead around and into the center of the space. An iron bench, placed directly in front of the urn, offers a place to sit.

> ADD DIFFERENT LEVELS TO YOUR PATIO BY CHOOSING PLANTS WITH UPWARD GROWTH HABITS. DRAW THE ATTENTION DOWNWARD BY PLANTING THOSE THAT TEND TO CASCADE.

A B O V E : A perfectly straight path made from cement tiles leads through this symmetrical space to a centrally placed sundial. All paths lead to the massive sundial, which in turn draws the eye upward, emphasizing the large scale of this garden room.

ABOVE: A steeply tiered rock garden incorporates stairways and paths constructed of flagstone. Grass and creeping herbs poke through the stones to soften their edges. Designed to have multiple points of interest, this slope features a central raised bed, a round metal table, a birdhouse, and a trio of tepees that provide support for climbing plants.

WHEN THE VIEW BEYOND THE GARDEN IS ALSO A FOCAL POINT, A LOW FENCE KEEPS IT IN SIGHT.

What's Underfoot?

An outdoor path should be surfaced with a material that is stable for walking and does not get slippery when wet. In general, an oft-walked path should be wide enough to accommodate two people at a time.

Paths may be hard or soft-surfaced; choose a material that complements the style of your outdoor space and the use to which you will put it. Some good choices include the following:

Hardscape paths are hard, durable, and need only minor maintenance:

Brick

Concrete pavers

Poured concrete (scored or patterned for traction)

Stone (choose a flat stone, such as flagstone or slate)

Softscape paths are soft, often made of natural materials, and require regular upkeep:

Wood chips or bark

Nutshells

Pea gravel or pebbles

Grass or dense ground cover

Hay or straw

RIGHT: Placed in a loose "two over one" pattern, these stone slabs form an elegant attractive walkway through a formal garden room.

LEFT: Concrete pavers carve a path through a densely planted flower bed that forms the passage from the street up to the front door. A walk through the flowers makes for a pleasant journey that sets the tone for the home.

A B O V E : An exquisite example of a *parterre* garden room features a cross-shaped pathway made of red brick and patterned concrete slabs. The path converges at the central point, where an old well-turned-planter holds court.

IN A FORMAL GARDEN, WHERE SYMMETRY REIGNS, UNUSUAL DETAILS ADD INTEREST. TWO NEOCLASSICAL URNS IN THE FORE-GROUND MEET AN UNEXPECTED MATCH IN A DUO OF CONTEMPORARY TERRA-COTTA POTS THAT FLANK THE BENCH.

LEFT: Stone slabs anchor a path made of woodchips that leads into an outdoor alcove designed to showcase the subtle beauty of foliage. Branches edge the path, gently holding back the growth.

BELOW: A splendid garden room planted for maximum color effect requires a pathway that will blend in subtly— here, tan gravel fits the bill. The wide walkway guides visitors along the flower bed, leading them to a wooden bench from which to enjoy the view. Once they have savored the colorful garden, they may notice, tucked in among the plantings, a salvaged stone arch, perhaps once home to a stone figure, but that now sits mysterious and empty among the flowers.

A B O V E : A rustic garden room devoted to showcasing flea-market
treasures uses a candle-lined brick path to lure guests from one
destination to the next.

A B O V E : The destination at the end of this path is a charming
guest cottage. A winding walkway made of brick pavers leads the
eager guests forward, but not so directly that they lose the
opportunity to admire the little house's architecture.

Freestanding Structures

Freestanding structures, such as pergolas, arbors, gazebos, and sheds, can be among the loveliest and most inviting of outdoor rooms. At once beautiful and functional, they may be open, "virtual" rooms or actual walled and roofed rooms. These garden structures, which come in a wide array of styles, share certain characteristics that make them so appealing.

The architecture of columns and posts lends vertical punctuation to spaces that are often mostly flat. Roofs, partially open to the sky or fully closed, offer shelter as well as the sudden pleasure of an invitation to an intimate space or passageway. Cutout shapes are perfect for framing views, and they tempt vines and climbers to twine through.

The arbor, with its arched top, makes a particularly inviting gateway that can be used as an entrance to a space or to enhance a passage from one area to another. The pergola, with its open woodwork "roof," dates back to the ancient Egyptians—offering dappled or full shade, it forms an excellent canopy under which to dine or relax outdoors. Gazebos, cupolas, and sheds—all more substantial yet still (usually) small in scale—provide real shelter and outdoor storage.

Adding this kind of architecture to an outdoor space, as the photographs in this chapter reveal, is a fabulous way to transform the landscape and redefine the mood.

A CHANDELIER CAN HANG FROM A STOUT BRANCH TO ILLUMINATE THE TABLE AND FURTHER BLUR THE DISTINCTION BETWEEN INSIDE AND OUT.

L E F T : A wide iron arbor forms a dramatic arched entry to an outdoor dining platform set under a massive maple tree. With its upper rails wreathed in wisteria, the arbor draws the eye upward, creating a transition from the open lawn up the sandstone stairs to the high leafy "ceiling" of the dining room.

ABOVE: A fabulous custom-built arbor is reminiscent of a Victorian four-poster bedstead. With wide, built-in benches on three sides, it has room for a table in the center. Tree-trunk posts and branch details give the arbor a rustic expression; plenty of comfortable cushions create a relaxing, inviting ambience. Thickly twined vines shelter the entire structure from the elements.

RIGHT: A zigzag pathway takes a turn beneath an iron arch draped in roses and clematis. The riot of colorful flowers spilling from the top of the arbor brings a touch of exuberance to this well-mannered and carefully trimmed space.

L E F T : A large pergola on the lawn gives shelter to an outdoor dining table and support to a hammock laden with cushions. The stone table, with its pedestal base, anchors this outdoor room and imparts an air of permanence.

A B O V E : An old garage provides a sheltering wall and a pretty backdrop for this outdoor dining area. Where a driveway once began, a rose arbor now leads to a colorful gathering of potted plants that surround a dining table. A candelabra is suspended from a tree to illuminate evening meals.

Garden Architecture

Though many of these terms are used interchangeably, they do have specific meanings. Here is a brief guide to the most common garden structures.

Arbor: An open shelter of wood, metal, or plastic with latticework sides and top, crowned with an arched or flat roof.

Bower: An arbor made solely of entwined plant material.

Trellis: A lattice that forms square or diamond shapes; frequently made of wood or plastic.

Pergola: A framework with posts or columns supporting a flat, open roof of girders and crossbeams, usually made of wood.

Cupola: A dome-like structure.

Gazebo: A freestanding, roofed structure that is open on all sides.

USE A COMBINATION OF OUTDOOR LIGHTING TO PROVIDE EVENING ILLUMINATION: CANDLES, TORCHES, AND LANTERNS CAN BE STAKED INTO THE GROUND WHEREVER LIGHT IS NEEDED.

RIGHT: A seasonal outdoor dining space takes shape beneath a colorful cloth affixed to four posts wedged into the earth. In this charming spot, various vintage finds come together to make a delightful summer room. Two old garden benches flank a sturdy wooden table graced with a floral cloth.

LEFT: A row of evenly spaced arbors creates a colonnaded corridor leading to a rustic garden bench. Thickly growing vines curtain the arches, and lushly planted beds line the walkway, creating a sheltered, intimate atmosphere.

GARDEN ACCESSORIES WITH A PURPOSE, SUCH AS SUNDIALS AND BIRD-HOUSES, LEND MEANING TO AN OUTDOOR SPACE.

ABOVE: Marking the end of a walkway and the beginning of a grassy lawn is a broad iron arbor with a canopy of roses.

REGULAR PRUNING IS ESSENTIAL TO KEEP A LIVING PASSAGEWAY OPEN— GETTING TANGLED IN THE VEGETATION RUINS THE EFFECT.

LEFT: A dense hedge with a cutout archway forms a shady bower, a romantic spot to stop and contemplate the path ahead.

RIGHT: A gentle slope overlooking a meadow offered an ideal location for this expansive tree-branch arbor, which organizes the entire outdoor space into a beautifully framed composition. The overhanging vines shelter a dining room from which the view in any direction is equally delightful.

LEFT: Part gazebo and part garden shed, with gothic arches and rustic branch materials, this unique structure is an appealing blend of styles and functions. It provides a visual anchor for this end of the garden, a vertical counterpoint to the beautifully executed *parterre* centered on the brick patio. It also includes a sheltered bench offering relief from sun or rain, as well as storage for garden tools.

A REPEATING VISUAL MOTIF ADDS MEANING TO THE DESIGN; HERE, THE TABLE AND CHAIRS FEATURE GOTHIC ARCHES TO ECHO THOSE OF THE SHED.

RIGHT: A cupola transforms a potting shed into the image of a quaint Victorian cottage. The English garden theme is carried through in the white picket fence and abundant cottage-style garden.

USE ONE EMBELLISHMENT TO DRAW ATTENTION TO THE NEXT. THIS TRUMPETING ANGEL ENCOURAGES VISITORS TO LOOK UP TOWARD THE CUPOLA, WHICH IS CROWNED WITH A BALL FINIAL.

A B O V E : A passionate collector of garden antiques has turned a potting shed into a diminutive museum housing a lifetime of finds. A jumble of formal and rustic pieces, the elements all come together in the embrace of a low hedge.

LOW-GROWING BUT DENSE HEDGES MAKE EXCELLENT BOUNDARIES. FOR A CLASSIC LOOK TRY BOXWOOD, PRIVET, OR YEW.

ABOVE: An outdoor room for the cooler months, this greenhouse is as attractive as it is functional. Weathered paint gives it a pleasantly well-worn feeling in keeping with the casual patio. Filled with light and plants well before spring has fully bloomed, it is a welcome winter sanctuary.

L E F T : In this woodsy setting, a leaf-entwined pergola on a brick patio offers a secluded and sheltered spot to situate a semipermanent outdoor dining room. The feeling of the room can be altered by the choice of linens and tableware—a white cloth accompanied by crystal and silver serving pieces lends a formal air; a bare table and paper plates would make for a more casual but no less enjoyable meal amid the trees and flowers.

A B O V E : With a structure to grow on, plants can create living walls that offer privacy and seclusion. Here, a cedar arbor boasts a dense covering of roses that forms a natural "roof," while a boxwood shrub anchors the base of each column. The result is an intimate seating area that can be used for relaxing or dining.

Impromptu Rooms

Ultimately, desire is the only true prerequisite for an outdoor room. It does not require a lot of empty space or an existing porch, deck or patio; it does not need an unforgettable view or any architectural elements: all that is needed is the urge to make a comfortable outdoor refuge.

An impromptu outdoor room happens when you yield to this urge and establish an actual space specifically intended for outdoor living where none was before. You can make it as simple or as elaborate as you wish; your impromptu room might be a leafy alcove fitted with a single chair or a full dining room with seating for twelve. It can incorporate elements already existing in your yard, from the substantial and fixed—trees, outbuildings, and hedges, for example—to the transient and portable, such as potted plants or garden furniture. Alternatively, your impromptu outdoor room can be an on-the-spot creation born simply from transporting indoor furnishings outside. The trick is to make use of whatever is at hand to design a bit of actual living space outdoors—temporarily.

A place to sit is the minimum requirement for an impromptu room; a place to eat is also nice. Anything beyond may add more convenience, extra comfort, or greater beauty—but is not strictly necessary.

If the ease of outdoor living works its magic on you, however, you may find that there is no obstacle to bringing more and more of your indoor accoutrements outside. You may also discover a desire for a more permanent outdoor room.

An impromptu room, however, is for seizing the moment—it may last a season, a weekend, or a couple of hours. It's up to you.

LEFT: A folding table and chairs swiftly transform a small backyard into nature's own breakfast nook, with an orange tree proffering its fruit for fresh-squeezed juice.

ABOVE: Off to one side of the path from the house, screened by plants, this hammock swings gently in the shelter of a sturdy tree and is a favorite place to relax.

CONTAINER PLANTS CAN BE EASILY MOVED AROUND TO FORM A TEMPORARY BOUNDARY.

LEFT: An irresistible site under a tree was the inspiration for this agreeable impromptu dining spot. A worktable covered with white cloths makes a pleasing table and two benches dragged outside for the day provide seating. The potting table has become a sideboard.

R I G H T : A comfy wicker rocking chair, positioned at just the right spot to take in the sights and scents of the roses in the fading afternoon sun, turns the yard into a purely relaxing personal space. A tray holding a drink within arm's length is a pampering touch.

R I G H T : A vantage point with a view of the water is always a special location. On a calm day, a picnic table can be moved onto the dock and covered with a flowing blue tablecloth. Add just-grilled burgers and corn-on-the-cob, plus a bucket of fresh blooms, and a casual barbeque turns into a special event.

LEFT: A tree by the lake presents a pretty site for an outdoor birthday party. Dappled sunlight filters through the branches, under which a long farmhouse table is dressed up with a diaphanous cloth. Carrying everything down to the picnic spot is easy with a big gardening basket.

ABOVE: At the border between backyard and woods is a perfect place to find solitude and serenity. Two stout trees provide the anchors for a simple rope hammock—and a haven in which to spend many relaxing hours is created.

Hammock How-Tos

To properly hang a hammock, you need two sturdy anchor points. These could be two trees, two posts, a wall and a post or tree, or most easily, the posts of a hammock stand.

• The distance between your anchor points should be approximately a foot (30 cm) longer than the hammock itself; lay the hammock flat and measure between the suspension rings to find your hammock's length.

• Trees should be a minimum of a foot (30 cm) in diameter. Posts should be at least 4 inches (10 cm) square.

• A hammock with spreader bars should be mounted at least 4 feet (1.2 m) above the ground; one without spreader bars should be hung at least 6 feet (1.8 m) up.

• Never attempt to get into a hammock feet first. Turn around and sit down on the hammock, then hoist your feet up.

LEFT: On a pleasant evening, why not dine outside? Here, an autumn banquet is the event that has called for an outdoor dining room. A tree curtained with Spanish moss is the backdrop; a long, sturdy table covered with a plain white cloth is laid out with a magnificent feast.

A BUCKET PACKED WITH ICE MAKES A SIMPLE, PORTABLE BEVERAGE HOLDER.

RIGHT: The pleasing sound of splashing water sets a celebratory mood, making this spot on the lawn overlooking the fountain the ideal location for a summer afternoon party. A folding table is layered with gingham for a dressy look, the repast is set out, and the party is about to begin.

A SPARE TABLECLOTH IS A HANDY ACCESSORY IN AN OUTDOOR ROOM, WHERE IT CAN DO DOUBLE DUTY AS A PICNIC BLANKET OR BE DRAPED OVER A HANDY TREE TO GIVE SOME SHADE.

L E F T : In fine weather, an elegant living room is extended to the outdoors. The upholstered settee and armchair, plus a small table, transform this patio into an outdoor parlor. The home's architecture, featuring tall windows and dentil moldings along the roofline, is a dramatic and fitting backdrop for this formal room.

A B O V E : Surrounded by a white picket fence, this hilltop pasture overlooking the trees is a splendid spot for a gathering. To facilitate the event, an outdoor rug has been laid down (note how it defines the space) and a collection of comfortable pieces have been moved outside to accommodate the partygoers. The cushioned chairs and sofa ensure that everyone can enjoy the fresh air in comfort for a nice, long while.

ABOVE: When the afternoon sun gently shines through the trees at the far end of the backyard, it is time to create an intimate outdoor conversation nook next to a wall of flowering hydrangea, by simply placing a pair of folding chairs in a corner of the lawn.

WHEN SETTING UP HEAVY FURNITURE ON THE GRASS, INSERT TILES BENEATH THE LEGS—THEY WILL PROVIDE A FLAT SURFACE ON WHICH TABLE AND CHAIRS CAN BE STABLE.

LEFT: A pear tree marks the spot for an impromptu outdoor dinner on this expanse of green lawn. A farmhouse table, informally set and surrounded by a bench and folding chairs, makes a fine dining area.

Bring the Indoors Out

One of the elements that makes an impromptu outdoor room feel so special is the delicious, almost rebellious feeling evoked by bringing furnishings usually found indoors out. A chandelier, hanging from a tree, for example, makes an evening gathering feel magical. If the outdoor area has electrical wiring, an extension cord may be all that is needed; a candle-powered light is even easier and can be hung almost anywhere. Here are some other ideas:

• An area rug instantly defines a space. A new trend is the all-weather rug, which is available in styles ranging from Oriental to modern, and can even be left outside. If you're sure the weather will hold, bring out an indoor area rug.

• Upholstered furniture always seems more elegant than furniture obviously created for outdoor use. Carry out chairs and a sofa to create a sense of cozy intimacy in the yard.

• Mirrors are wonderful additions to the outdoor space. Depending on where they are placed, they can reflect and expand the sky, the view, or the light (day or evening), offering a different perspective on an otherwise familiar space.

• Artwork, not just sculpture and statuary, but even paintings, can be brought outside to add a special touch.

Any of these items can instantly help to create a beautiful outdoor room where none existed before.

RIGHT: A wrought-iron chandelier adorned with glass embellishments sparkles above this table.

ABOVE: A perennial border defines this yard; within it is a small, personal shady oasis created by placing a wrought-iron chaise longue under a garden umbrella. A small side table completes the scene. Since all the pieces are easily moved, this little impromptu space can be made to appear wherever and whenever desired.

RIGHT: A romantic vision resulted in this exquisite canopied sanctuary for two rising up from a long, rolling span of unremarkable lawn. Tent poles, rope, and muslin are the materials required for the canopy; its borders are emphasized by the potted roses set at each corner. Beneath it, two rustic benches are made more comfortable with the addition of throw pillows and blankets. A candlelit chandelier signifies the intent to linger well into the evening.

MASON-JAR LUMINARIA CREATE A TWINKLY PATHWAY.

Photography Credits

Page 1: Charlie Colmer
Page 2: Jeff McNamara
Page 3: Steven Randazzo
Page 5 top: Steven Randazzo
Page 5 middle: Andre Baranowski
Page 5 bottom: Janet Loughery
Page 6: Donna Griffith
Page 8: Paul Draine
Page 10: Keith Scott Morton
Page 12: Gridley & Graves
Page 14: Jessie Walker
Page 15: Gridley & Graves
Page 16: Andre Baranowski
Page 17: Saxon Holt
Page 18: Jonn Coolidge
Page 19: Colin McGuire
Page 20: Ericka McConnell
Page 21: Gridley & Graves
Page 22: William P. Steele
Page 24: Lisa Sacco
Page 25: William P. Steele
Page 26: Steven Randazzo
Page 28: Roy Gumpel
Page 29: Michael Luppino
Page 30: Steven Randazzo
Page 32: Ericka McConnell
Page 33: Keith Scott Morton
Page 34: Keith Scott Morton
Page 37: Keith Scott Morton
Page 38: Steven Randazzo
Page 39: Keith Scott Morton
Page 40: Robin Stubbert
Page 41: Saxon Holt
Page 42: Keith Scott Morton
Page 43: Keith Scott Morton
Page 44: Andre Baranowski
Page 46: Michael Luppino
Page 48: Keith Scott Morton
Page 49: Keith Scott Morton
Page 50: Keith Scott Morton

Page 51: Donna Griffith
Page 52: Grey Crawford
Page 53: Grey Crawford
Page 54: Grey Crawford
Page 55: Keith Scott Morton
Page 56: Rob Melnychuck
Page 58: Keith Scott Morton
Page 60: Lynn Karlin
Page 61: Lynn Karlin
Page 62: Keith Scott Morton
Page 63: Lisa Sacco
Page 64: John Glover
Page 65: Grey Crawford
Page 66: Gridley & Graves
Page 68: Keith Scott Morton
Page 69: Jessie Walker
Page 70: Michael Luppino
Page 71: Keith Scott Morton
Page 72: Hotze Eisma
Page 74: Ray Kachatorian
Page 75: William P. Steele
Page 76: Gridley & Graves
Page 77: William P. Steele
Page 78: Gridley & Graves
Page 80: John Peden
Page 81: Lynn Karlin
Page 82: Donna Griffith
Page 83: John Glover
Page 84 top: Rick Wetherbee
Page 84 bottom: Gridley & Graves
Page 85 top: Saxon Holt
Page 85 bottom: Mark Lohman
Page 86: Janet Loughery
Page 88: Lynn Karlin
Page 89: Rick Wetherbee
Page 90: William P. Steele
Page 92: Marianne Majerus
Page 93: Keith Scott Morton
Page 94: Richard Felber
Page 95: Ray Kachatorian

Page 96: John Peden
Page 97: Chuck Baker
Page 98: John Glover
Page 99 top: Rick Wetherbee
Page 99 bottom: John Glover
Page 100: Gridley & Graves
Page 101: Jessie Walker
Page 102: Colin McGuire
Page 104: Keith Scott Morton
Page 105: Keith Scott Morton
Page 106: William P. Steele
Page 107: Jonn Coolidge
Page 109: Kate Gadsby
Page 110: Keith Scott Morton
Page 112: William P. Steele
Page 113: Marianne Majerus
Page 115: William P. Steele
Page 116: John Glover
Page 117: William P. Steelc
Page 118: Rob Melnychuck
Page 119: Donna Griffith
Page 120: William P. Steele
Page 121: William P. Steele
Page 122: Keith Scott Morton
Page 124: Ryan Benyi
Page 125: Chuck Baker
Page 126: Ray Kachatorian
Page 127: Debra McClinton
Page 128: Helen Norman
Page 129: Keith Scott Morton
Page 130: Alan Richardson
Page 133: Keith Scott Morton
Page 134: Jeff McNamara
Page 135: Keith Scott Morton
Page 136: Helen Norman
Page 137: Charles Maraia
Page 139: Ann Stratton
Page 140: William P. Steele
Page 141: Ann Stratton

Index

Note: Page numbers in *italics* refer to illustrations